Charles Charming's Challenges
on the Pathway to the Throne

CLIVE JAMES

Charles Charming's Challenges on the Pathway to the Throne

A Royal Poem in Rhyming Couplets
with illustrations by Marc

JONATHAN CAPE
THIRTY BEDFORD SQUARE LONDON

First published 1981
Text © 1981 by Clive James
Illustrations © 1981 by Marc
Jonathan Cape Ltd, 30 Bedford Square, London WC1

British Library Cataloguing in Publication Data

James, Clive
Charles Charming's challenges on the
pathway to the Throne.
I. Title
821   PR9619.3.J27
ISBN 0 224 01954 6

Printed in Great Britain
by St Edmundsbury Press
Bury St Edmunds, Suffolk

To George Russell

Agamus igitur pingui Minerva, ut aiunt.
Cicero, *De Amicitia*, V

Nor I hope will it be considered presumptuous for a man of low and humble status to dare discuss and lay down the law about how princes should rule; because, just as men who are sketching the landscape put themselves down in the plain to study the nature of the mountains and the highlands, and to study the low-lying land they put themselves high on the mountains, so, to comprehend fully the nature of the people, one must be a prince, and to comprehend fully the nature of princes one must be an ordinary citizen.

Machiavelli to Lorenzo de' Medici
in *The Prince*, translated by George Bull,
Penguin Books, 1970

A GUIDE TO THE CHARACTERS ON THE PATHWAY TO THE THRONE

CHARLES CHARMING, Prince of Wales, heir to the throne.

ELIZABETH II, Queen, and mother to Charles.

PRINCE PHILIP, Duke of Edinburgh, father to Charles.

SIR CECIL BEELINE, a photographer.

PRINCESS MARGARET, aunt to Charles.

CRAWFIE, a pest.

GROUP CAPTAIN PETER WETEND, DFC, a suitor.

QUEEN SALOTE OF TONGA, a red-hot mama.

RICHARD DIMBLEDON, a rotund broadcaster.

PRINCESS ANNE, sister to Charles: a centaur.

PRINCE RANDY, brother to Charles: a satyr.

TONY, EARL OF NIKON, another photographer.

CHRISTIAN BARNYARD, a surgeon.

KRAUT HUN, a teutonic pedagogue.

LADY JANE WELLYBOOT, loyal friend to Charles.

QUEEN ELIZABETH THE QUEEN MOTHER, grandmother to Charles.

SIR ROBERT GORDON MENSROOM ('MING'), Prime Minister of Australia.

SIR HAROLD WILES, Prime Minister of Great Britain.

GAFFE LAMEWIT, another Prime Minister of Australia: a giant.

MRS LAMEWIT, wife to Gaffe: a giantess.

KERRY PACKMULE, best friend to Charles: a schoolboy.

THE MAYOR OF BONDI, an Australian public official.

LORD BUTTERBALL, a go-between.

OLD MAC McHACK, an institution.

SIR ANCIENT STATELY-HOME, a listed building.

PROFESSOR FREDDIE SPARE, an amorous
   philosopher.
RAYON WOOLLENS, a radical.
PROFESSOR ISRAEL BLINTZ, a polymath.
F. R. LOOSELEAF, a prophet.
DAME HELEN GARDENOME, an inspiration to
   women.
A. J. P. TAILSPIN, an historian.
LOULOU, a courtesan.
DES COXCOMB, another broadcaster.
ESTHER HOTPANTZ, yet another broadcaster.
UNCLE DICKIE, a paragon.
RODDY, a gardener.
THE KENTS, royal extras.
THE OGILVIES, more royal extras.
BARBRA STRESSBAND, a virago.
SIR DOUGLAS BAYBOMB, an ace pilot.
THE DUCHESS OF WINDSOR, a socialite.
THE GUINNESS GIRLS, a dance group.
PRESIDENT NICK DIXON, a moral example.
TRICIA, daughter to Dixon.
WILLIE HECKLETHRONE, MP, a watchdog.
ARCHBISHOP COGWHEEL, a rebarbative divine.
MALCOLM MOTHERMILK, a saint.
DAVID DROSS, a phenomenon.
ALAN WHANKER, another phenomenon.
ST-JOHN STILTHEELS, a fop.
LORD LUCAN, a mystery.
LADY HARDHART, a hostess.
JIMMY GOLDCAP, a publisher and tycoon.
LORD LAMBCHOP, a flâneur.
ANGIE RIPEMOV, a newsreader.
TINA VON BRAUN, an editor.
LADY FREESIA FRUITCAKE, a biographer.
HAROLD HALF-PINT, an elliptical playwright.
RICHARD INKWELL, a satirical editor.
WILLIAM DENS-FOGG, another satirical editor.
HARDY AIMHIGH, a tailor.
DR OWNUP, a right-wing Labourite.

SHIRLEY WHIRLEY, another of the same.

ROY JUNKET, a Councillor for Social Democracy.

MARGO HATBOX, Prime Minister of Great Britain.

BAUBLES HAMSTRUNG, a roly-poly bundle of good fun.

LORD FATMAN, a sage.

TITO, a kit of spare parts.

JOHN PAUL GINGER, a polemicist.

MARK PILLOCKS, consort to Princess Anne.

DORLING WHITHERS, an equine commentator.

FARRAH FAWCETT-DOWNWARDS, a picture of health.

LADY DIANA SEETHROUGH-SPIFFING, belle of the ball.

AND

King George VI, Greta Garbo, Queen Mary, John Brown, Sir Edmund Hillary, Mae West, the Goons, Shakespeare, Peter Sellers, John of Gaunt, the Black Prince, Peregrine Prykke, D. H. Lawrence, Lord Annan, Lord Snow, T. S. Eliot, Marcel Proust, Robert Browning, Elizabeth Barrett Browning, Donne, Chaucer, Albert Schweitzer, Mussolini, Hitler, Daladier, Sun Yat-sen, Gladstone, Christopher Wren, Dafydd ap Gwilym, Gareth Edwards, both the Biancas, all the Bonbon-Carters, Princess Marie-Astrid, Princess Caroline, Princess Grace, Errol Flynn, the Three Degrees, Brezhnev, Giscard, Prince Bernhard, Willy Brandt, Helmut Schmidt, Anna Pest, Lady Highrise of the Towers, Duff Gordon, Hannah Gordon, Gerald Ford, Anna Ford, Enoch Soames, Emma Soames, Jack Jones, Freddie Jones, Gemma Jones, Tom Jones, James Jones, James-Earl Jones, Ann Jones, David Jones, David Pryce-Jones, Dick Jiggle and many more.

EPISTLE DEDICATORY

Of you, the Prisoner in the Velvet Mask,
Amiability is all we ask.
All we require is that your every move
Should imitate the tin hare's in its groove.
Behind opaque and lockable front doors
We feather our own nests and snipe at yours.
No need to stipulate that you stand still
For mockery: we know full well you will.
Butt, hero, icon, patsy, plaster saint,
Our perfect gentle knight without a taint,
What luck you are what you're supposed to be!
We've got you where we want you, haven't we?

BOOK ONE

Of Life and Love and Liberty I sing
And of the PRINCE OF WALES our future *King*.
But *Wales* is not his last name. First things first.
At birth the boy was blessed, some might say cursed,
With the august surname *Charming*, family handle
Of Princes from *Cockaigne* to *Coromandel*,
Who all descend directly from a *Greek*
Ship-owning house of which I will not speak
Except to say that if you trace it back
To when the *Persians* sailed to the attack
At *Salamis*, you'll find the vivid sea
Signed with the honour of that dynasty
Who groomed their sons for marriage, not for
    slaughter,
And always steered towards the eldest daughter.
Suffice to note it was a *Charming* boy
Who wed ELIZABETH and brought her joy,
A fiery *Greek* with clean-cut *Danish* fair
Good looks, perhaps a wee bit short of hair.
His name was PHILIP. Proudly he now stood
Beside the crib and found the contents good –
A bright new flowering on a family tree
That went back to at least the *Odyssey*.
The KING and QUEEN had come to take a look
And leave a gift. It was a Ration Book,
For this was still the era of Austerity
When every luxury was still a rarity.
No wonder, then, news of the Royal Birth
Threw instantly a girdle round the Earth.
The fountains in *Trafalgar Square* ran blue.
The gutters in *Calcutta* did so too,
Or sort of blue. The *Empire* might and main
Strove to forget that it was on the wane.

(13)

The future *Queen* had had a son. A cheer
Went up that you can practically still hear.
Their tot, the doting parents were agreed,
Must be called CHARLES, plus all the names he'd
    need
To satisfy heraldic protocol –
In other words enough to fill a scroll.
I'd like to list them, but there'd not be room
If I raved on until the crack of doom
Like *Moses'* monologues in *Deuteronomy* –
And anyway, my watchword is economy.
Likewise a man of few words, *Philip* spoke.
'Thank *Christ* that's over. Sturdy little bloke.
Bit short of chin, perhaps. Still, you can't tell.
Right sort of food, might turn out bloody well.'
Propped up among the pillows, weak with joy,
His wife declared:
                    'We're *so* glad it's a boy.
The Monarchy's a man's job in our view,
Though when our turn comes we dare say we'll do.'
And on she twittered in the Royal plural.
In those days no one got an epidural
And though she'd taken pleasure in her pain
She'd found the whole thing something of a strain.
At this point CECIL BEELINE, not yet knighted,
Came shuffling on. He looked a bit short-sighted.
'Oh *Lilibet*,'
            he cried,
                        'I've never seen
A Princess looking so much like a Queen.
The queens I've known have generally been men.
But you'll soon be a *real* Queen! What fun *then*!
And on your feet already! My, what strength!
And there's your husband lying down full length.
That negligee! He looks *so* sweet, my dear!
And this must be the baby over here.
Delightful skin! Like *Garbo*, my old flame.
Now watch the birdie. Say cheese. What's *your*
    name?'

(14)

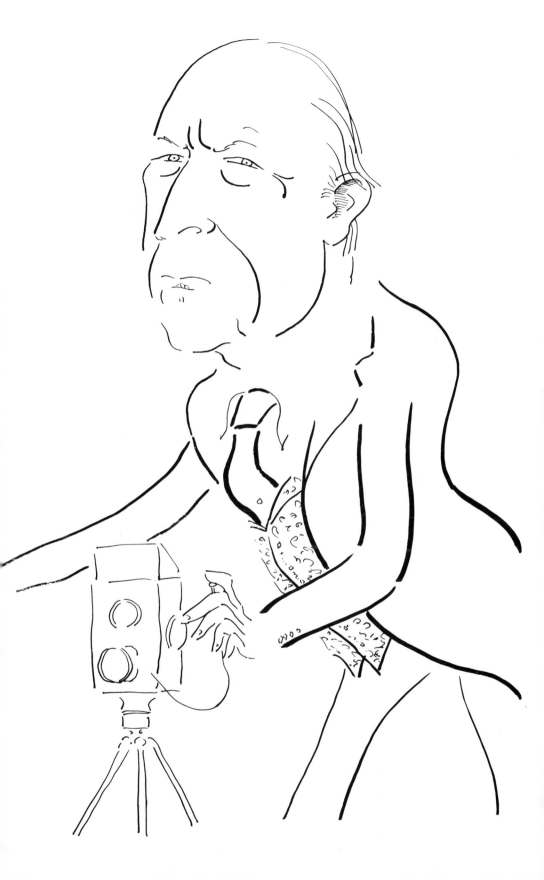

He photographed a corgi with great care.
Elizabeth looked on with fond despair
And knighted him. He blinked away his tears
And raced off to start spending thirty years
As that delightful stuttering old nutter
Sir Cecil Beeline, First Knight of the Shutter.
By now towards the *Palace* had come swarming
The whole world, but the gates withstood the
    storming.
They swung aside, their bear-skinned guards saluting,
Only when challenged by the silver fluting
Of *Daimler* grilles. Hoarse cries of
                                    'Here they come,
God bless them!'
                    paved the way for the *King*'s Mum,
Queen Mary, likewise *Princess Margaret Rose* –
And *Crawfie*, too, had followed her keen nose,
Infallibly attracted to the spot
Where with discretion she could spill the lot.
Queen Mary in her usual gracious style
Bestowed on everyone her tiny Smile.
She smiled at faithful servants one and all,
She smiled at suits of armour in the hall,
She smiled at her dear *Lilibet*. Some chap
Came to attention and took off his cap.
Oh yes! The husband. *Philip*. That was it.
Names tend to slip when you get on a bit.
But look at this! Yes, every inch a King.
With any luck she'd see the christening,
Provided it was not delayed too long.
From front on, the child's chin looked almost
    strong . . .
Margaret, meanwhile, stood at the window. Two
Hot tears slid down her cheeks, for there he flew,
So close that she could touch him, yet so far –
The man the rules had placed out of her star,
Group Captain Peter Wetend, DFC.
He zoomed around defying gravity
With victory rolls and other aerobatic

Manoeuvres he thought suitably ecstatic,
But underneath the wings over his breast
His noble heart was cracking in his chest.
His *Hurricane* fell like a falling leaf
And spiralled upward like a sob of grief.
With canopy pulled back it made a pass
At stalling speed so low the back yard grass
Turned dark with prop-wash. So he waved farewell
While *Philip* bellowed:
                                        'Blast and bloody hell!
That noisy blighter's curdled my wife's milk!'
But at that moment *Wetend* hit the silk.
His plane had clipped a statue of *John Brown*
With its port wing-tip and turned upside down:
The sad *Group Captain* somersaulted clear
And drifted off along the atmosphere,
And with one last, lost gesture he was gone –
Puffed by the breeze into oblivion.
But *Margaret*'s lonely vigil was made brief
By being caught up in a general grief.
She and the other Royal women soon
Perforce wore mourning morning, night and noon.
The *King* was dead. Long live the *Queen*. The rain
Fell softly into *London* like the grain
Of some old photograph in black and white.
The glass streets were long mirrors full of light
As down them the gun-carriage slowly rolled
Drawn by young ratings capless in the cold.
The pipers played '*My Home*', the foot guards
   marched
With arms reversed and every throat was parched
Despite the fact that every cheek was wet.
But why evoke what no one can forget?
Unless, of course – please say it isn't true –
You weren't alive in 1952.
But everyone was, weren't they? Anyhow
Prince Charles was, and that fact will do for now.
For now, down the same streets, but in warm
   weather,

A different procession altogether
Hove into view, with e'en the humblest varlet
Clad in a panoply of gold and scarlet,
While what the nobs wore might have made a bird
Of paradise feel just a bit absurd.
The drumsticks danced in pairs. The *Queen of Tonga*
Led all the younger crowned heads in a conga,
While those too old to show a pair of heels
Shook to the rhythm of the carriage wheels.

The Golden Coach went by. The *Queen* inside it
Was radiant and did not try to hide it,
For following the Coach came ample proof
Of her intention not to be aloof.
It was the Golden Pram. Pushing with pride,
The faithful *Crawfie* modified her stride
To match the progress of the Coach in front
And so avoid the least hint of a shunt.
The *Prince*, meanwhile, employed his small right
    hand
In ways the world had learned to understand
Might be regarded as the Royal Wave.
The sight sufficed to make the groundlings rave
Despite the fact his arm moved half an inch
As if controlled by pulley, wire and winch.
The *Queen*'s Own Gesture echoed by her child
Did weird things to a crowd already wild:
They hugged each other sinking to their knees,
Whole families toppled backwards out of trees,
While RICHARD DIMBLEDON announced the Dawn
Of a New Era.
                'Something has been born
Today. A New *Elizabethan* Age.
New figures have begun to take the stage.
New hopes. New aspirations. *Everest*
Has just been conquered by the very best
Type of young man. *Sir Edmund* did not flinch
As day by day and painful inch by inch
The *Sherpas* piggybacked him to the peak.
And now I'm with young *Charles*. Perhaps he'll speak
About this great new mood of victory
We're all so moved by at the *BBC*.'
But *Charles*, who at that time was barely four,
Could only say:
                'One's not exactly sure
One can fulfil one's role. One lives in hope
That in the long run one will learn to cope.'
And thus his life of sacrifice began
Long, long before he grew to be a man.

(19)

BOOK TWO

The *Empire* shrank but few cared. If *Charles* grew
    That was enough to justify the New
Elizabethan Age, which proved indeed
To be a fine time for the *British* breed
But not because their power increased: far from it.
The flag came down as often as the *Comet*
On country after country. What was good
Was how the people broadly understood
The time had come to give back with good grace
The *Empire*'s lion's share of living space
And learn to live within their limitations
As just one in a Commonwealth of Nations.
The *Fleet Street* Lords absorbed the lesson last
But with the *Suez* boob they caught on fast
And prated less of military might,
Shifting the emphasis to Moral Right –
Which concept it's a *British* native oddity
To treat as an exportable commodity.
Thus *Britain*'s role aspired to the symbolic
Which made the *Queen*'s task almost apostolic.
She rose to the occasion, as we know,
Though it might easily have not been so.
Unfettered by parameters statistical
Her world-wide influence was well-nigh mystical
And just because one woman was called Royal
Whole countries were delighted to stay Loyal.
The point, she saw with prescient acuity,
Was to maintain the cherished Continuity
While always being ready to Adapt.
Thus centuries of precedent were scrapped
And *Charles* was sent to school, just as if he
Were made of common clay like you and me.
Not yet the *Prince of Wales*, young *Charles* was
    known

By his subsidiary names alone.
It was as the mere *Duke of Cornwall* then
That he, plus his small escort of armed men,
Arrived so unobtrusively to start
The new term at *Hill House*. Set in the heart
Of *Knightsbridge*, from now on this institution
Drew crowds as if a public execution
Were taking place inside it every day –
Which was just what was happening, in a way,
Since *Charles* soon found his struggle to fit in
Was the one battle he could never win –
The fight was lost before the fight began
And he must spend his life as a marked man.
Great-Grandma died, which left him short of friends
At court, the kind on which a chap depends
If that chap's mother happens to be *Queen* –
With not much time left over from routine.
His sister *Anne*'s arrival was a plus
Although there was not much one could discuss
With her as yet. *Anne* thought it a good game
To crawl backwards and forwards past the same
Poor sentry till he'd wrecked himself saluting –
And when he fell face-down she'd crawl off hooting.
Charles disapproved, but *Anne*, unlike her brother,
Was like her father more than like her mother –
Impulsive. None the less she came in handy
To divert Press attention, as did *Randy*
When *he* arrived. So full marks to the stork;
But still it was a long and lonely walk
To school, and when they switched the school to
     Cheam
His waking hours became one long bad dream,
Since every living soul except the Press
Shunned him to prove how they could not care less
That he would one day sit upon the Throne –
Just one more thing he'd have to do alone.
'One finds',
               he mused,
                         'what makes it hard for one

Is that one can't complain. It isn't done.'
Made glum beyond his years by such grim thoughts
He ferried home a clutch of school reports
Which showed his general progress to be small –
And maths he simply could not do at all.
His pocket money, which did not amount
To much, he couldn't really even count,
Since any coin resembled any other –
They all seemed to be portraits of his mother.
When TONY, EARL OF NIKON, came to visit
The school, he kindly said:
                                        'Not easy, is it?
The minute that I married your Mum's sister
I started missing being just plain Mister.
At least, though, I once knew what it was like:
But as for you, you'll never know, poor tyke.
Your parents sent you this.'
                                        It was a boat,
The one he'd asked for. Smallest boat afloat
On the school pond, it wanly dipped along
While *Charles* kept to himself his sense of wrong,
But in his letters home the odd pale blot
Tipped off the *Queen* that things were not so hot.
'It troubles us to see our son and heir',
She pondered,
                        'in the grip of such despair.
This letter strikes us as a cry of pain.
It looks as if it's been out in the rain.'
The *Duke* stared through the window at the pink
Stretch of the *Mall* and had a quiet think.
'Soon make a man of him at *Gordonstoun*,'
Said *Philip* with a lightening of his frown.
'Cold baths. A bit of PT. Climb a cliff
Naked at night. If they don't like it, biff!
Touch of the rope's end or the old belt buckle
About the bum. Good crack across the knuckle
Works wonders. When they find out that it hurts
To hang on, they let go of Mummy's skirts
Damned quick. It won't take long to break him in.

But first we'll have to stiffen up that chin.'
At this *Her Majesty* looked apprehensive.
Cosmetic surgery was still expensive
In those days, and there had been certain cases
Of people coming out of it with faces
Worse than they had gone in with. The *Duchess*
Of Marlborough before last – a frightful mess.
'Well, yes,'
                    the *Queen* sighed,

                              'we suppose we must
Allow it. Is there someone we can trust?'
The short-list *Philip* held held just one name.
CHRISTIAN BARNYARD had not yet soared to fame,
Nor would he till he first transplanted hearts:
But having cut his teeth on other parts,
Already he was known in certain quarters
As one who could change ugly duckling daughters
To swans by simply shuffling certain bits,
And many a great châtelaine now sits
On pads of flesh that elsewhere on her torso
Once made her look like *Mae West* only more so.
'Clinic's in *Zurich*. Might as well get him',
Prince Philip rasped,

                              'to give *Anne*'s nose a trim.
Two birds, one stone. We'll pack them off tonight.'
And off he went to line up the *Queen's Flight*.
A *Heron* left *Brize Norton* after dark.

Both *Charles* and *Anne* thought this a terrific lark.
They liked the secrecy – that precious stuff
Of which they never seemed to get enough,
Although, of course, they were not yet aware
That all their lives it would grow still more rare.
But now they drowsed, and then they fell asleep,
And by and by their sleep grew very deep,

As *Barnyard* stood above them in his mask
And delicately set about his task.
'Go easy, son,'
                    he told himself,
                                        'one slip
And beck we go to *Efrica* by ship.
Might even have to walk. Here's the first slice . . .
And there's the cartilage. Yes, thet looks nice.'
The end of *Anne*'s nose with a little saw
He cut off and transferred to *Charles*'s jaw.
Brilliantly simple, but it all took hours.
What taxed him to the limit of his powers
Was putting in the thousand tiny stitches.
Even today when *Anne*'s lost tissue itches
Charles scratches it, to soothe the phantom lesion
Left by the adjunct's method of adhesion.
But really, since the scars are subcutaneous,
To raise these minor quibbles is extraneous.
Success was overwhelming from the first.
The *Queen*, prepared as always for the worst,
Took one look at the poor bruised black and blue
Façades of her two darlings and she knew
That they would heal into a fresh perfection –
The interfering hand defied detection.
'We're very pleased',
                        Her Majesty declared,
'To see these irritating faults repaired.
A blemished Royal profile rather cramps
The style of those chaps who design the stamps.'
'Now *Charles*,'
                barked *Philip*,
                                    'when you get to school
For *Christ*'s sake please observe this golden rule,
Or else you might be on a sticky wicket:
By all means rub your new chin but *don't pick it*.'
'Good luck, dear,'
                    said the *Queen*.
                                        'Oh, by the way:
We've made you *Prince of Wales* as from today.'

BOOK THREE

The *Heron* vanished southward, leaving only
The *North Sea* cliffs, a small boy looking lonely,
And tall beside him, tanned by wind and sun,
The principal of *Gordonstoun*, KRAUT HUN.
'He still flies good, your father,'
                         Hun declared.
'Best boy I ever had here. Never scared.
One time I towed his whole class out to sea
And told them to swim home in time for tea.
He was the only one got back alive.
Maybe he ate the others. We survive
By learning to look danger in the face:
That way we purify the human race.
I see from the report they send from *Cheam*
They made you captain of the soccer team
The only year it never scored a goal.
Forget all that. I teach you self-control.
We start right now. You see that row of huts?
That is the school. Let's see if you got guts.
The path we're on is booby-trapped and mined,
So you go first. I won't be far behind.'
Charles gulped but set off bravely through the maze
Of trip-wires glinting in the evening haze.
The compound was surrounded by a moat:
You had to cross it in a rubber boat
Which gradually deflated as you paddled.
Charles found his noble brain becoming addled
But clung hard to a log, which only later
Revealed itself to be an alligator.
By that time, though, the *Prince* was home and dry
And being shown the dorm. A little cry
Of fear escaped him when he saw his bed.
Was this where he must lay his Royal head?

'From now on,'

              sneered *Kraut Hun*,

                             'you sleep on nails.

An *Indian* idea which never fails
To keep the drowser free from dreams of loose
Behaviour, not to mention self-abuse,
Which should he even try it he would tend
To make a waffle-iron of his rear end.
Not that Your Highness ever would be tempted.
Such urges are, however, best pre-empted.
You sleep now. In the morning, a cold shower
And then fall in near the machine-gun tower.'
Next day on the assault course poor *Charles* found
That being *Prince of Wales* gained him no ground.
Quite the reverse. His class-mates did their best
To make a torment out of every test.
They double-greased the ropes from which he swung.
They half sawed through the rungs to which he clung.
He wiped his nose and found it running blood.
He sighed and spat a mouthful of cold mud.
And all this before breakfast, after which
They playfully tossed him into a ditch.
His hair all spud-peel, gravy and sweet corn
He surfaced wishing he had not been born,
But instantly despair turned to resolve.
With hardened heart he vowed he would involve
Himself in all the manly pastimes going –
Determined he would make a decent showing.
'One simply must',

              he mused,

                         'accept one's fate.

One can't expect the whole thing on a plate.
One simply has to learn to grin and bear it.
It's just a case of if the crown fits wear it.'
Impressed, they helped him bathe and change and
    then
They picked him up and threw him in *again*.
Thuswise the months of pain turned into years
With every night spent on his nails in tears,

But no one ever heard a single sob
As doggedly he got on with the job.
On visits home not one word of complaint
Escaped his lips, although he felt quite faint
With envy at *Anne*'s licensed concentration
On the minutiae of equitation.
The few meals she did not take in the stable
She fed her ponies at the dinner table
While *Randy* in a pedal car gave chase
To every female servant in the place –
The *Palace* rang with his horn and Anne's hoot
While *Charles* sat glum, save when *Jane Wellyboot*
Dropped in to see him in his *Beatle* wig.
He writhed and strummed. The act went over big
With her at least. She'd tap her foot and clap.
'This sort of girl appreciates a chap,'
Thought *Charles*.
                    'If only one could stay down here
And make mass entertainment one's career
And be a *Goon* and sing the *Ying-tong* song
And tour the world and *Jane* could come along.'
But back flew *Charles* each time to the far North,
That fearful frith beyond the *Firth* of *Forth*,
That landscape of bald rocks and slimy crags,
The home of shagged-out clams and clapped-out
    shags.
(I think that's a Rhetorical Device
I've just used – anyway it felt quice nice.)
By now *Charles* had attained the dizzy rank
Of *Guardian*, for which he had to thank
His own tenacity and *Hun*'s belief
In heaping hardship on a future chief.
In other words the lonely little bleeder
Who once had looked so lost was now a Leader
Responsible for stroking home his crew
And all the other things that leaders do.
Charles felt more trapped than ever, so no wonder
He led his lads into a frightful blunder.
Fog caught them on the cliffs. A pub was handy.

(29)

Hot drinks all round. His was a cherry brandy.
The place of sin looked cut off by the mist.
Inside, however, sat a Journalist,
Who watched *Charles* drain his glass and set it down
And then got on the telephone to town.
A storm blew up that never quite blew out.
The whole world talked about his drinking bout.
For *Fleet Street* the event was Heaven sent.
They flogged

THAT CHERRY BRANDY
INCIDENT

For all that it was worth, which was of course
Nothing at all, since even a dead horse
Must first have lived. The tabloid press, however,
Makes up with crassness for not being clever.
The billboards went berserk week after week.
Charles was called home but found the prospect bleak.
'One couldn't face the *mater* or the *pater*,
Not in the circs,'
        he muttered.
                  'Perhaps later.
Just now one simply couldn't stand the quarrel.
Meanwhile one's *Grandmother* is at *Balmoral*.'
That night the young *Prince* dodged from hut to hut
Between the searchlight beams and deftly cut
His way out through the wire. He swam the moat
And scampered through the minefields like a goat.
Next day he and his *Grandmother* caught trout
Almost as fast as they could pull them out.
Fly-fishing was the *Queen Mum*'s favourite sport
And all she had to teach, *Charles* had been taught.
They stood knee-deep in water so like air
Only the ripples told you it was there.
The fish flew through it inches off the ground
And shuttled back and forth before they found
A fly to swallow. It was suicide.
Nevertheless they died pop-eyed with pride.

'My *Bert* was one and you look like another:
Too human for the job,'

                              said the *Queen Mother*.
'But niceness doesn't get you off the hook.
Remember, though: You Are the Way You Look.
You've got the acting talent. Half the art
Of being Royal is to play the part.
Start off by putting strangers at their ease
With Royal Opening Remarks like these.
"Have you come far?" They always like that one.
And always ask how many years they've done
Whatever thing they do the whole day long –

Your hands behind you and you can't go wrong.
Pretend to be a Prince. Your *Grandpa* wept
When *David* did a bunk but he still kept
The bargain. Not that he had any choice –
And he had nothing like as good a voice
As you have. Chin up. He that plays the King
Will one day *be* the King. The play's the thing.'
The annual *Shakespeare* play put on at school
Most often featured *Prince Charles* as the Fool.
But now, in his last year, he snared a role
Appropriate to his unfolding soul.
It was *Macbeth*. He practised by the hour
The talk and walk and look of kingly power.
He strode around with hands behind his back
Endeavouring to cultivate the knack
Of looking like somebody to be feared
Despite a cardboard sword and crêpe hair beard.
The night arrived and he was pretty good.
Hands clasped behind, he greeted *Birnam Wood*.
'Have you come far?'
                              he asked in Royal fashion
But *Banquo*'s spectre most aroused his passion.
'How long',
                he queried,
                              'have you *been* a ghost?'
The *Queen* and *Duke* were there.
                              'Don't like to boast,'
Barked *Philip*,
                'but the boy's a treat to watch.
Let's hope he doesn't take a swig of Scotch.
He's copied me. Tell by the way he stands.
I like that thing he's doing with his hands.'
'We must say we're impressed,'
                              the *Queen* concurred,
'We're hanging on our offspring's every word.'
The line that might have drawn unwanted laughter –
'All hail *Macbeth*, that shall be King hereafter' –
Aroused a cough or two but nothing worse,
Such is the grandeur of the *Bard*'s blank verse.

BOOK FOUR

Although his place at *Cambridge* was well earned
Some subtle things young *Charles* had not yet
   learned.
His parents thought he needed Finishing.
But at what school? At this point in stalked MING,
Sir Robert Gordon Mensroom of *Australia*,
Knight of the *Thistle*, *Grand Duke* of the *Dahlia*
And *Lord High Gladioli*. Silver tongue
Still working well and portly *poitrine* hung
With all the chains and tokens that denoted
A *Warden* of the *Sink Plug*, *Ming* emoted
Thuswise:
                    'Your Majesties, if you'll permit
The Liberty, I'll gladly do my bit
To help you give young *Charles* that final burnish
Even the finest diamond needs. We furnish,
At our great school called *Timbertop*, facilities
Not only to bring out a boy's abilities
But to impart that quintessential air,
Compounded of *sang-froid* and *savoir-faire*,
Which in my country always has surrounded
Those few by whom the many are astounded.
Myself for instance. Note the self-assured
Hauteur by which my enemies are floored,
The gloss which to the voters means so much –
And yet I never lose my common touch.'
Exemplifying democratic ease
Ming mouthed this whole oration on his knees,
And ever and anon bent down and kissed
The Royal slipper, which he sometimes missed,
Whereat the stippled Wilton met his lips
And had its nap sucked up in little sips.
The *Queen* and *Duke* across his bobbing stern

Exchanged a glance which he could not discern
But which he otherwise might have construed
As tempering disgust with gratitude.
'We think the scheme ideal,'

                  announced the *Queen*.
The *Duke* agreed.

             'Must say I'm bloody keen.
He needs that cool no-nonsense kind of poise
He'll only get when he's One of the Boys.
That's why the *Aussies* make such good equerries.
They're arrogant as *Frogs* and fight like *Jerries*.'
While this was being said *Ming* was still bowing,
Salaaming, genuflecting and kowtowing.
They tactfully suggested he efface himself.
Discovering yet more ways to abase himself,
He backed off down the long reception room
And slowly disappeared into the gloom
Of History's Antipodean annexe.
The next man to be shown in wore a *Gannex*
And smoked a pipe. His name was HAROLD WILES,
Prime Minister of *Britain*. Ghastly smiles
Of bogus welcome strained the Royal features,
Inspired by this most *déclassé* of creatures.
'Let me be frank',

         Wiles said,

                'about your son.
No, please don't interrupt. I've just begun.
The Coal Board would be more than pleased if he
Could follow the example set by me
And join them as a prestige figurehead.'
'You handle this,'

         Prince Philip bluntly said
And left his wife to cope while he got started
On helping *Charles* to pack. The *Prince* departed
Within the hour aboard the prototype
Concorde, which like a cinematic wipe
Translated him abruptly round the planet –
The trip stopped opposite where he began it,
And out he fell to find the bright sky filled

By GAFFE and MRS LAMEWIT.
                          'We're real thrilled
You're giving *Timbertop* a burl, Your Grace,'
Said *Gaffe*,
              'Cause it's a bonzer little place.
Allow me to present my lady wife.'
The sheltered *Charles* had never in his life
Seen anyone to equal these two giants,
Whose monumental stature baffled science.
Their heads were usually obscured by cloud,
But not today, for now they gently bowed
And reached down to squeeze *Charles*'s tiny hand
And make him welcome to the Great South Land.
'Give us a tinkle if you want a feed,'
Said *Mrs Lamewit*.
                    'Looks as if you need
A bit of building up. You off your tucker?
Here comes a kiss.'
                    Charles saw her great lips pucker
But had not time to move aside before
He felt himself sucked upward with a roar.
His head began to spin and did not stop
Revolving till he got to *Timbertop*.
The bouncing of the litter brought him to
In time to be astonished by the view
Of mountain peaks protruding through the mist
Sent up by breathing tree ferns. From one wrist
He plucked a leech, and from one ear another,
And gulped wet air and felt that he might smother.
The native bearers set him crudely down
Beside a bark hut. In a dressing gown
And sandshoes, with his face as yet half shaved,
A hulking brute who looked like a depraved
Prizefighter shambled out and growled:
                                        'G'day.
I hope them boongs weren't too rough on the way.
Name's KERRY PACKMULE. Glad to have you here.
I'm Captain of the School. You want a beer?
Your Grace is hereby welcomed to Down Under.

(37)

Charles is a poofter name. I'll call you *Chunder*.'
Despite his more than twenty years at school
On certain subjects *Kerry* was no fool.
He showed young *Charles* the art of chopping wood
And kept him at it till he understood.

The white chips flew, the heap of wood grew high,
While *Kerry* stretched out on a stump nearby
And dreamed aloud of plans to make the game
Of cricket less traditionally tame.
'The day that my old man drops off the twig,'
Mused *Kerry*,

        'I'll be on to something big
As far as cash goes. Struth, the *Pope*'s a *Jew*
If I can't blue all that on something new.
The whole game needs a good kick up the arse
Combined with my good taste and touch of class.'
At this point *Charles* froze. Prostrate on a branch
A creature lay whose aspect made him blanch.
Its scaly skin had a metallic sheen,
Its length and pulsing plumpness were obscene,
Its blue tongue fluttered like a battle banner.
'Relax,'

    said *Kerry*,

        'only a goanna.
Don't worry about lizards, for *Christ*'s sake.
But if it's got no legs then it's a snake,
Like that one near your foot. You'd be a wreck
If *he* got on to you. Hold on a sec.'
While *Kerry* lazily picked up an axe
Charles had a series of small heart attacks.
He closed his eyes and heard the sudden whistle
Of metal and the crunch of severed gristle
And then a yell from *Kerry*.

        'Shit a brick!
You'd better get those toes sewn back on quick.'
Charles spent the next week in the matron's tent
And found out what *Australia* really meant
In terms of insect life. Beset by flies
And fleas he lay there uttering weak cries
Of anguish which were lost among the noise
Kicked up by all the other suffering boys
Who lay around him. No one else in fact,
Apart from *Kerry*, had survived intact
A single term. The school's whole population

Had been reduced to some form of prostration,
Most often brought about by living things
Which came equipped with hypodermic stings.
One boy who'd fallen in a bull ants' nest
Was understandably a bit obsessed.
A fortnight later he was still hysterical,
His throbbing body absolutely spherical.
Another boy had put on his slouch hat
But had not, until too late, noticed that
The hat contained the sort of centipede
Which hates confinement very much indeed.
Before they started bandaging his head
He first had to be buckled to the bed.
Yet *Charles* preferred the scene, although *Infernal*,
Inside the tent to anything external,
For outside lay yet more of the same feral
And floral focal points of painful peril
That had reduced him to his present state.
Suave *Kerry* reassured him.

                      'Listen mate,
No worries. Just be careful in the dunny.
A red-back up your arsehole isn't funny,
Believe me.'

          Charles believed him, but evinced
A certain vagueness even as he winced.
'One's not quite certain what a red-back does,'
He ventured.

             'Does it hum, or does it buzz?'
'Gawd struth,'

        cried *Kerry*,

                 'don't come the raw prawn!
You Pommy poofters hardly know you're born.
Red-backs are spiders. Get one up your bum
You'll more than likely end up deaf and dumb,
So always take a dekko down the pan
Before you drop your strides. That's if you can:
You can't if it's too dark, but then the red-back
Is blind too: you can sit there with your head back
And look up at the stars all night and dream

(40)

Of picking *Kerry Packmule*'s Cricket Team.
I think I'll go there now and squat. Feel free
To come and have a mag. That's where I'll be.'
Grateful for *Kerry*'s visit, *Charles* declined
The offer, but the thought was on his mind.
The night wore on while he fought off the urge
To go forth in the dark and stage a purge.
By rights the thought of *Kerry*'s red-back warning
Should have postponed his promptings until morning.
Alas, his disciplined digestive tract
For once was restively resolved to act.
With spiders rife in his imagination
He groped and stumbled through the vegetation
Until he bumped into the rough-hewn seat
Of what he sought. With trousers round his feet
He strove to quell the visions in his mind
Of spiders poised to jump up his behind,
But soothingly a soft voice from close by
Drew his attention to the brilliant sky
In which each constellation was a cluster
Of diamonds revelling in its own lustre –
Pendants and brooches, necklaces and sprays
All overlapped in one triumphant blaze.
'Them stars up there have got what I want. Light.
I'll bung my cricket matches on at night.
I'll paint the balls black and the stumps and bails
A nice bright red to match the players' nails.
Crash helmets will protect the head and face
And also provide advertising space
By means of small revolving neon signs
Promoting leading brands of beers and wines.
The batsman's boxes will have pink propellers.
The wicket-keeper will be *Peter Sellers*.
The umpires will wear tutus and high heels.
I might replace them with performing seals . . .
I'm sick of this place, *Chunder*. Let's shoot through
At sparrow's fart. I'll tell you what we'll do.
We'll hitch a lift to *Melbourne* and then fly
To *Sydney* and go surfing at *Bondi*.'

(41)

This book has had an excremental theme
So far, and though *Bondi* looked like a dream
Of sun and sparkling water and clean air,
I fear the boys were not free even there
From cloacal preoccupations. Lumps
Of fecal matter floated, forming clumps
Which rose like rafts into the booming breakers
To be distributed through foaming acres.
The sewage came from further up the coast.
Charles staggered out the colour of pot roast.
The MAYOR OF BONDI had arrived to meet him
But *Charles* gave that poor man no time to greet him.
'One might as well be swimming in the loo,'
Said *Charles*.
               'One's very deeply in the poo.'
'If we'd known you was coming, you mug lair,
We would have stopped the pumps,'
                          averred the *Mayor*.
'Now don't',
         snapped *Charles*,
                     'come the raw prawn with *me*.
Just get in there and clean that flaming sea.'
While *Mayor* and *Corporation* armed with spade
And bucket made a dutiful parade
Of purifying the putrescent ocean,
Young *Kerry* gazed at *Charles* with deep emotion.
'You've come on, *Chunder*,'
                     he announced with awe.
'In no time you'll be laying down the law
To all them poofters you was born to rule.
I reckon this is your last day of school.'
Two friends whose paths through life must shortly
   part,
The silent boys shook hands with heavy heart.
They stood picked out in solemn silhouette
Against the sea the sun lit as it set,
A hot pink disc that hissed with a terrific
Finality into the cool *Pacific*.

BOOK FIVE

In *Cambridge* there is only one front gate
Fit to receive a future Head of State.
To *Trinity* belongs the proudest portal
That ever made a man feel merely mortal.
The painted scutcheons poised above the doors
Make you inclined to enter on all fours.
They boast of *John* of *Gaunt* and the *Black Prince*
And almost everyone before or since
Who ever led Crusades or conquered *France*
Or would have done if he had had the chance.
By now, with his new aura of authority,
A candidate to join this bold minority,
Prince Charles, with movements languid but effective,
Accompanied by his alert detective,
Stepped from his car before his new front door.
Two thousand frantic press-men with a roar
Converged on him and bore him to the ground.
The poor detective still has not been found
To this day. That young *Charles* survived the scrum
Was no mean tribute to his new aplomb.
Inside the gate LORD BUTTERBALL stood smiling:
A manatee's attempt to look beguiling.
Between the jowls and just above the chins
The mouth curved in the weakest of weak grins;
Beneath the lower eyelids puffs and sags
Of flesh formed matching sets of battered bags;
But nothing really touched the eyes themselves
For soulfulness. They wobbled on their shelves
Like water-filled balloons. A silent bleat
Of longing for a lost *10 Downing Street*,
His gaze remembered how *Old Mac McHack*
Had somehow crept around behind his back
And with one piercing blow had sealed his doom.
And that was how *Sir Ancient Stately-Home*

Became *Prime Minister*, while *Butterball*,
His expectations dished beyond recall,
Dragged his slow girth to this great Seat of Learning
For years of walnuts, port and pointless yearning.
But one good part was still left to be played
Which gained from being played out in the shade:
The role of Moral Tutor to the *Prince*.
The *Prince* was gladly testing out the chintz
Armchairs in the first room he'd ever known
Where he could count on being left alone
Instead of merely lonely – which is not
Quite the same thing by any length of shot.
It did the world of good to sport his oak,
Get dressed for bed and have a quiet smoke.
Night fell. With happy weariness imbued
He sat enjoying his new solitude.
Just then he saw the most amazing thing
Vaguely occur amongst the panelling.
Without a sound a door-shaped void had yawned
In which *Lord Butterball* now stood and fawned,
The bobble on his nightcap hanging down
Below the hem of his drab dressing gown,
While lower still his ancient leather slippers
Were so worn they looked like a pair of kippers.
'Useful device. Through this I can appear
And nobody will know that I've been here
To give you what informed support I can
In my capacity as Grand Old Man.
I framed the Education Act, you know:
That's why you're here. Pity it had to go,
The world as it once was, but there you are.
Or rather here *you* are. You keep a car?'
'One understood that cars were not allowed,'
Said *Charles*, a bit awed, not to mention cowed.
'Hang on to yours,'
          said *Butterball*.
                   'We'll bend
The rules a bit. Look on me as a friend.
Two years from now you'll sit for your degree

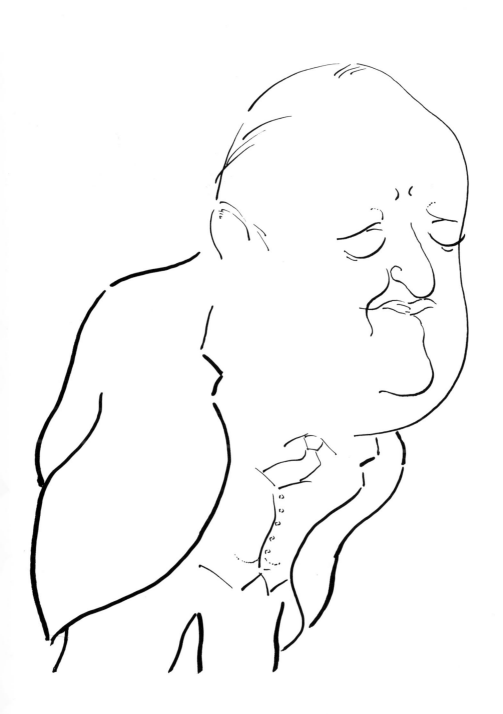

In Anthro-whatsit-arco-pology.
Till then there's time for broadening the mind
By access to the best brains you can find.
Some are in *Oxford* but we'll bring them to you.
I'm feeling a bit tired. You don't mind, do you?'
Lord Butterball crept into *Charles*'s bed.
His snores were loud enough to wake the dead.
By morning *Charles* was numb from lack of sleep
And truth to tell he thought it a bit steep
That he should be so ill-prepared to face
The fastest talker that the human race
Possessed, *Oxford*'s PROFESSOR FREDDIE SPARE.
At 9 a.m. precisely *Spare* was there
In *Charles*'s doorway and already talking,
Something he also did while he was walking
Or lying down or (so the story went)
Bestowing the most heartfelt compliment
A brain like his could pay to femininity –
The fleshly act of spiritual affinity.
'Good, good. You've got your pen and paper ready.
But what does "good" mean?'
                         asked *Professor Freddie*.
'The pen and paper we can verify,
Or anyway I can. But who am I?
Or, rather, *what* am I? Ghost or machine?
Must you be here to find out what I mean?
Who *are* you, incidentally? Rings a bell,
That face of yours. I know that face quite well.
I had lunch with the *Queen* last week. Relation?
She fancied me, of course. That information
Is strictly between us, you understand.
I felt her shiver when I kissed her hand,
Poor creature. But what do we mean by "feel"
If we do not mean "know"? Are feelings real?
Well, come on, come on, come on, try a guess.
Think, *think*! That's it! You're thinking! Yes, yes, yes!
It's trembling on your tongue! Speak, speak, lad,
    speak!
Alas, time's up. Must dash. Same time next week.'

(47)

And in the doorway which had featured *Freddie*
Was nothing but an eerie, airy eddy.
But no respite. A bell struck ten past nine
And punctually appeared the next in line.
His name was RAYON WOOLLENS, come to teach
Some form of politics. Earnest of speech,
In mode of dress he was no whit less grim.
The Trendy Left could lay no claim to *him* –
His Leftness harked back to an older school
As stubborn as a mule and grey as gruel,
A stagnant pool of glutinous viscosity
Where failed polemics foundered in pomposity.
'You represent a Ruling Class attempt',
Droned *Woollens*,

                'to behave as if exempt
From Social Thrusts by which Manipulation
Becomes habitual to the population –
And yet you form in fact part of the Flow
By which a given television show
Resembles any other . . .'

                  On he canted
Of how the helpless masses are implanted
With standard patterns of response, and yet
To *Charles* it seemed of all the men he'd met
That this man's patterns of response were more
Standard than anything he'd heard before,
As well as tedious beyond belief.
The bell, thank goodness, kept the session brief:
Off shuffled *Woollens* in his roll-neck sweater
To write a book and thus make the world better.
The Pedagogues' Parade went on and on
As each few minutes don succeeded don
While *Charles* took notes with scarcely time to munch
The sandwich he was sent in lieu of lunch.
PROFESSOR ISRAEL BLINTZ appeared before him
And instantly such waves of verbiage bore him
Backwards into the room that he at first
Thought some enormous water-main had burst.
In point of fact *Blintz* had just said hello.

(48)

But here was *Woollens'* daft idea of Flow
Made actual in one man, whose every word
Was joined to the word after. Thus you heard
A verbal seamless garment. Consonants
Piled up so fast they left vowels little chance
To breathe, and poor *Prince Charles* no chance at all
As he stood pinned by sound-waves to the wall.
'KERENSKYTHOUGHTSHOULDBEACONSTITUTION,
BUTBOLSHEVIKSBELIEVEDINREVOLUTION.
FORLENINLIBERALISMWASCHIEFTHREAT,
TERRORTHEMEANSBYWHICHTHREATMUSTBE
  MET . . .'
But why go on? Suffice to say our friend
Stayed upright till the bell declared an end,
Whereat another don and then another
Came on while *Charles* received them like his mother
Beset by embassies from foreign lands
With foreign papers clutched in foreign hands.
What F. R. LOOSELEAF in full flow was like
Readers will know who've read my *Perry Prykke*,
So here I will restrict myself to saying
That *Charles* found his whole attitude dismaying.
'The *Bloomsbury* network *Lawrence* so detested',
Growled *Looseleaf*,
                'for support finally rested
On Royalty and all that that implies
By way of cocktail parties, old school ties,
Smart friends and the debilitating glitter
Which understandably made *Lawrence* bitter
When he, with his organic sensibility,
Combined with what I might call his virility,
Remembered what this country once had been.
The fate of *Eliot* shows what I mean –
The mantelpiece weighed down with invitations,
The wearing of black tie, the coy flirtations
With items of prestige like the OM,
Which *Lawrence* did not get. Not to condemn
Such triviality is to condone
The Blind Enlightened Menace which alone

I grappled with when all those Against Life
Called me a crank. Except, of course, my wife,
Who stood beside me helping me to edit
The only publication which did credit
To *Cambridge* when *Lord Annan* and *Lord Snow*
Were at the *Palace* – this, I think, you know –
With cocktails in each hand and dinner jackets
And colour supplements and tennis rackets
And doing the *New Statesman* Competition
While I and *Lawrence* could not gain admission.'
The bell rang three times in the course of this
But *Looseleaf* was a hard man to dismiss.
At last, however, he was bumped aside
By one who was exceptionally wide
For one so small. She puffed up like a quail
And spoke like a canary in a gale.
DAME HELEN GARDENOME for all her laudable
Intelligence is scarcely even audible.
She drops so many names they form a heap
But what you mainly hear is:
                              'Cheep cheep cheep.
When *Tom* was (cheep cheep) writing *Four Quartets*
He told me (twitter) but (cheep) one forgets.
Not that *Marcel* (tweet tweet) forgot a thing
But then that was his thing, remembering.
Poor *Robert*, how he missed *Elizabeth*:
He never quite got (twitter cheep) her death.
I helped him cut *Sordello*. Twice as long
Initially. Where *John* (tweet tweet) went wrong
Was publishing *La Belle Dame Sans Merci*
Before he'd shown the manuscript to me.
Same thing (cheep cheep) with *William*. Half the plot
Of *Hamlet* (tweet tweet tweet) is tommy-rot.
He wouldn't listen. Stood (cheep) looking dense
As if (tweet) I was saying made no sense.
But *Geoffrey* couldn't (cheep) have (cheep) more sweet.
Cheep cheep. Tweet twitter twitter. Tweet tweet tweet.'
By this time day was done and *Charles* was too.
He listened to the last dons in the queue

(53)

With heavy eyes. A. J. P. TAILSPIN came
And went and poor *Charles* would have felt the same
If he'd not come at all, since what he had
To say was all so brilliant it was mad.
'If *Albert Schweitzer* had been *Chancellor*
Of *Germany* there still would have been war,'
Said *Tailspin* while his tie gaily revolved.
'The situation had to be resolved
And *Mussolini, Führer* of the *Reich*,
Resolved it, using methods not unlike
Hitler's in *Italy*. Meanwhile in *Russia*
Daladier, like *Sun Yat-sen* in *Prussia*,
Was finishing what *Gladstone* had begun.
Is this where I switch back to camera one?'
Charles couldn't tell if *Tailspin* was insane
Or he himself had suffered a strained brain.
He rolled his oak shut with his last reserves
Of strength and poured a drink to calm his nerves.
Dusk gathered in the window leads. He dressed
For bed and on his gas-ring cooked the best
Meal he could manage. Most of it was stew
Brewed from a tin of the cubed kangaroo
His old friend *Kerry* sent him by the crate.
At last he lay down. It was very late,
So he at first was not delighted when
He saw the secret panel gape again.
He blinked. A woman of some kind stood there
Attired in what must be lace underwear.
Another don, he guessed. What did she teach?
She looked all plump and juicy like a peach.
Perhaps she taught gymnastics. Something physical.
He sat up feeling strange and looking quizzical.
'*Lord Butterball* sends you his compliments,'
The girl announced.

                'Should you be feeling tense,
He thinks perhaps a massage might relax
Those knotted muscles. Yes, you see? Your back's
All tight. Let's rub it. So's your neck and chest.'
So, it appeared, was nearly all the rest.

(54)

'My name is *Countess-Princess Louloubelle*
La Bomba di Prosciutto-Kunstwerk dell'
Annunziata-Cheeseburger van Fleet,
Archduchess of Coblenz and Ancient Crete.
Just call me *Loulou*. No, you put that here,
Not there. I think you'll find that that's my ear.'
'One likes this subject very much indeed,'
Sighed *Charles*.
                    'One thinks this is the one to read.'
'It isn't on the course,'
                    breathed *Loulou*.
                                        'Now
Shut up a minute while I show you how.'
She showed him. Using all her tactile skill
She put her willing pupil through the mill.
He groaned and giggled, wriggled and revolved,
He writhed, rotated, dithered and dissolved.
The Heir Apparent to the *British* Crown
Spent half the evening hanging upside down.
Without quite knowing what all this was for
The weary *Charles* kept coming back for more.
At last, with few clues what it was about
But well content, he quietly passed out,
A new taste on his young tongue as he dreamed –
And in his sleep he licked his lips and beamed.

BOOK SIX

One day of *Charles*'s life just took a book.
Excessive, but we had to take a look
In detail at his hurricane induction
Into the apparatus of instruction.
Now we can skip a bit. No need to dwell
On how the leaves turned brown before they fell
And how around the Library built by *Wren*
The lawns turned white and then turned green again,
As calico that's first bleached and then dyed
Spreads the more smoothly, being mollified.
The seasons came and went – that's no great news.
I'd show more tactlessness than you'd excuse
If I should add that once you've seen them do it
In *Cambridge*, then you know there's much more to it
Than physical phenomena arranging
Themselves in changeless sequences of changing.
The fructive breath of spring, for instance, brings
The girls out floating past the back of *King's*
Like sprays of lilies. Drifting punt by punt,
Poled by some spotty and straw-boatered runt,
They part the water-kissing willow tree
Past *Clare* and *Tit Hall* down to *Trinity*.
Charles saw such fragrant boatloads gliding by
And thought how much he'd like to have a try.
No hope, for *Fleet Street* would be on the scene
By hydrofoil and midget submarine
Before he'd so much as put in his pole:
He'd have to stick to polo, on the whole.
He sighed and turned and sat down with his cello
To bow a simple melody but mellow,
Suggesting, with its elementary purity,
The bitterness beneath his new maturity.
The average undergraduate could waste

His time in any way that met his taste.
Not so the *Prince of Wales*, who was denied
A space to breathe in or a place to hide.
One night he and his armed guards got back late
And found the bolt shot on the College gate.
'Good show! One's always wanted to Climb In,'
Said *Charles* with an expectant, moonlit grin.
He led his bodyguard, enjoined to caution,
Off through the dark to find the hallowed portion
Of wall where gentlemen by long tradition
Effected a discreet late-night transition
From outside where cold proctors lay in wait
To inside where hot coals lay in the grate.
Charles rubbed his chill hands and got set to climb
But did no more than that before his time
Ran out. A battery of floodlights blazed
So brilliantly the flintstone walls looked glazed.
Sirens went off, bells chimed. A two-ton van
Drew up from which men vaulted and began
Assembling with amazing speed a flight
Of marble stairs that climbed through the white night
To where *Lord Butterball* stood on the roof
Shaking his august head in fond reproof,
While various attendants and divines
Made gestures on the same indulgent lines.
A plush red carpet unrolled down the stairs.
Charles mounted heavy-hearted while fanfares
Of welcome were unleashed from trumpets long
And straight and unrelenting in their song
Of triumph. Thus the heralds cracked their cheeks
While *Charles* feared this might all go on for weeks
And wake up everyone for fifty miles:
So much for his big night out on the tiles.
But there was more. A mighty *thwack thwack thwack*
Was heard from high up where the sky was black.
A helicopter settled into view
Engorged with a whole television crew
Commanded by DES COXCOMB.
                                        'Man Alive',

He shouted,
    'asks: How can *Prince Charles* survive
A life spent subject to such scrutiny?
To help us put that question, here with me
Is ESTHER HOTPANTZ. *Esther*, it's your cue.'
'*Well, Des*,'
   piped *Esther*,
      '*I* agree with *you*.
I think that *all* this *fuss* is pretty *mad*.
Look at him, *cowering* there. He's *just* a *lad*,
A *baby* like *this* one I'm holding *here*.
That's it. Drink up your *milk* now. *There's* a dear.'
Her breast and teeth bared like a mock Madonna
She sat aloft with every eye upon her
While *Des* like a new *Joseph* drunk with pride
Crouched signing cheques and contracts at her side,
And all below looked up with ruffled hair
To see them in their element, the air:
A Holy Family held up by a hook
You can't quite see however hard you look –
Indeed such is that couple's awesome power
I've brought them on ere their appointed hour
To symbolise, by this conquest of space
And time, their unexampled state of grace.
From that day forth when *Prince Charles* walked
 abroad
He had the wherewithal to be ignored.
His escort would position a dustbin
And *Charles*, should the Press threaten, would climb
 in,
Thus finding some brief respite from his plight.
(The dustbin achieved fame in its own right:
At one stage a well-known front bench MP,
Today it's Chairman of the BBC.)
Charles also found it useful, when he spoke
In public, to unleash a Royal Joke –
Another way of hiding, since a jest
Of all means of concealment is the best.
The final term approached. To celebrate,

(62)

Charles asked his people up to dine in State
Chez lui on food prepared with his own hand
On his own gas-ring. The occasion, if not grand,
Was intimate. *Prince Philip* and the *Queen*
Sat on the couch. Perched on the fire-screen
Was UNCLE DICKIE, fully decorated:
Brass-bound, steel-lined, gold-studded, silver-plated,
Beplumed, bejewelled, emblazoned and embossed
With no thought for the weight or count for cost,
He was impervious to all attack –
Except, as we have since learned, from the back.
The *Earl of Nikon* squatted on the floor
While *Princess Margaret* hovered near the door
As if she would have rather been elsewhere
Where palm trees waved and salt spray thrilled the
   air –
The mystique-ridden island of *Mustique*
Where always it's the middle of next week
And young men make a fetish of the body,
And sing, and answer to the name of *Roddy*.
Anne, having left her horse somewhere outside,
Had found a fat chair-arm to sit astride
Which made her look a little bit less bandy,
While in the chair itself lolled the suave *Randy*.
The *Queen Mum* was there too, as were the *Kents*
And *Ogilvies*. It was, to all intents
And purposes, a Gathering of the Clan –
Part One of *Uncle Dickie*'s master plan
For making *Charles* a national cynosure
By means of a slap-up Investiture.
While *Charles* dished up a steaming vindaloo
Of curried rice plus *Kerry*'s kangaroo,
His Uncle with a tintinnabulation
Of medals sketched a Combined Operation
To equal his campaigns in the Far East,
Except the total cost would be increased.
'There's something going on that I don't like,'
He growled,
                   'the other side of *Offa's Dyke*.

The *Welsh* are getting restive. Time to prove
We care, before the swine get on the move.
Caernarvon, that's the spot. You see this map?
A ceremony. *Tony*'s just the chap
To do the frocks. *Charles*, learn the local lingo.
Those leek-eaters will go for it like bingo.'
The *Queen* with a sour look put down her fork.
'We understand that there has been some talk
Of bombs and things. We are not having that.
We're keeping him in *England* and that's flat.'
But *Charles* demurred.

                    'This is one's final term.
From now on one must serve the Family Firm.'
'The boy's right,'

            snapped the *Duke*.

                       'He's come of age.
His place is on the International Stage.
It isn't in the kitchen, that's for sure.
What *is* this bloody stuff?'

                   '*I'll* have some more,'
The *Queen Mum* said. *Charles* heaped food on her
  platter
While square-jawed *Uncle Dickie* clinched the matter.
'There's nowhere that the *Prince of Wales* can hide.
The tiger that he rides he rides with pride
Or not, but either way he can't dismount.
Someone once tried it but he doesn't count.
Now let's get going on the invitations.
Full speed ahead! No prisoners! Action stations!'
His epaulettes lit up. The silver stars
Massed on his chest spun round like bumper cars
While in amongst them other kinds of gong
Prismatically shed sparks or else went bong,
Ka-pweeng, clang-clang, zing-zing and rat-tat-tat
And streams of bubbles jetted from his hat.
On that theme there was no more to be heard.
The Family Strategist had said the word.

BOOK SEVEN

The dawning day of his Investiture
Found *Prince Charles* apprehensive and unsure.
Not that he feared the cloaked assassin's hand.
What scared him was his tenuous command
Of *Welsh*, which he had studied till his brain
Had turned to tapioca from the strain
With scant result. The few words he had mastered
Created the impression he was plastered.
A team of Druids was convened to teach
The *Prince* the fundamentals of their speech.
'Have you come far?'
                              he asked them. They had not.
Nor did his other question help a lot.
'How long have you been wearing those white sheets?'
They smoothed their seams and rearranged their pleats
And burbled on remorselessly in tones
That made them sound like mice with megaphones
While *Charles* strove might and main to comprehend.
They all played harps. They drove him round the
    bend.
Eventually no time was left. Depressed,
Charles started the long job of getting dressed.
A pair of velvet knickerbockers tied
Below the knee with silk ropes at each side,
A tunic made entirely of gold braid,
An arctic mink cape lined with pink brocade,
A pearl-encrusted platinum top hat
With *Prince of Wales* plumes perched on top of that –
All these went on in turn, until at last
With flies all buttoned up and flaps made fast,
He eased himself into his high-heeled shoes
And climbed on to his penny-farthing. Queues
Of druids in full livery lined the route:

Their harps went plunk, strange-looking pipes went
     toot,
While on the Castle lawn the Family Firm
Was gathered in such strength it made *Charles* squirm
With nervousness lest he let down the side,
And yet inside his head the gap yawned wide
Where his great speech in *Welsh* was meant to be,
And out there further than the eye could see
Were *Welshmen* standing shoulder to cold shoulder
Up hill, down dale and perched on every boulder.
With quailing heart he climbed down from his bike
And climbed the white stairs to the waiting mike.
The stairs were made of fibreglass. They led
Up to a plastic platform overhead
And down again, while fountains played and lines
Of dancing girls fleshed out *Nikon*'s designs.
Charles stood outlined against a brooding cloud
And nervously stared down into the crowd.
In unalloyed despair he searched his mind
And not a single *Welsh* word could he find.
He felt as if crosswires were centred on him.
Then sudden inspiration came upon him.
'Ying-tong,'
          he ventured,
                    'ying-tong Iddle-I-po.
Prestatyn Aberystwyth Llandudno.
I am the famous *Eccles. Henry? Min!*
Bluebottle Major Bloodnok Grytpype-Thynne!
Yes, folks! It's *Neddy Seagoon!* Hip hooray!
Carmarthen Merthyr Tydfil Colwyn Bay.'
The *Welsh* were overwhelmed. Such eloquence!
A blend of poetry and common sense
The likes of which they'd seldom heard before.
The Druids shivered, shaken to the core:
Dafydd ap Gwilym had not in his prime
Shown *Charles*'s gift for metre, tone and rhyme.
He spoke their language as if born to lead them.
Why, if they wrote him poems, he would read them!
The prospect dazzled. All fell there and then

To frantic plying of the bardic pen
While as a background to the scratch of quills
Such roars of adoration shook the hills
As were not heard when *Gareth Edwards* scored
His tenth try of the day. *Charles'* spirits soared.
His people loved him! At a prearranged
Signal from *Nikon* the stage picture changed.
The platform cut loose from the curving stair
And silently moved forward through the air.
While *Charles* stood imperturbably upright
Induction motors powered his eerie flight.
Borne onward in a kind of mobile stasis
He passed above a sea of upturned faces
Upon which rained a cataract of quips
And quiddities formed by his Royal lips.
He traced a giant circle round the town
And even as dusk fell did not come down,
For *Nikon*'s flares and rockets lit the sky
So brightly *Charles* was plain to every eye
Until the moment when he altered course
For *London* and like some triumphant horse
Who rounds the final turn into the straight
And tilting upright lets its stride grow great
He gathered speed so that his plumes blew back
And dwindled to a dot. The sky grew black
Reluctantly. A lone flare slowly fell
But in a short while that was gone as well,
And all the Royals climbed into their cars
And nothing lit the night except the stars.

BOOK EIGHT

The *Royal Navy* claimed the *Prince of Wales*.
The salt air heard the snap of swollen sails.
He grew a beard more vigorous than neat.
He learned to ply an oar and reef a sheet
And sheet a reef. Far out of sight of land
He learned first to obey and then command.
'Swab out the jib!'
                he cried,
                        'All poops abaft!
Lash down the foreskin and belay that shaft!'
His minesweeper went cruising in the *Med*.
It found no mines to sweep and so instead
It sailed around the world to *Hollywood*
Where Charles met BARBRA STRESSBAND.
                              'You look good
In that tuxedo, *Chuck*. Know what I mean?
Make sure you call me when they make you *Queen*.'
She led him off into a whirlwind dance.
Next day the whole world talked of their romance
But *Charles* had slipped away. Far out at sea
He pondered his unyielding destiny.
He dived on a deep wreck to find doubloons
But solitude eluded him. Platoons
Of other divers came down just behind him
And circled round as if sent to remind him
He was a treasure never to remain
Unguarded for an hour. Was it the pain
Of pressure in his ears that made him wince
When he came up? The next stop for the *Prince*
Was *Sandhurst*, where he rose up from the ranks
Until in no time he was driving tanks.
Leaving aside the fact it doesn't float
A tank is not that different from a boat,

(71)

So it was no surprise that *Charles* should make
The odd foray into a pond or lake.
'There seems to be',
                    he sighed,
                              'mud in one's gun.
How frightfully embarrassing for one.
One rather thought one was still sweeping mines.
You chaps look rather wet down there. Hard lines.'
Cranwell next stop. They taught him how to fly
But always stuck close by him in the sky:
Indeed his first instructor sat so near
That what he said was too loud to be clear.
SIR DOUGLAS BAYBOMB was the ace's name,
A name festooned with everlasting fame.
The *German* Air Force would not soon forget him.
He would have fought *Mugabe* if they'd let him.
He spoke the way he flew, with the authority
So crucial to our Air Superiority.
'That thing between your legs is called the stick.
You push it and you go down like a brick.
You pull it too hard and you might black out.
Just hold it loosely. Don't stir it about.
You got all that?'
                  Bemused, *Charles* said:
                                          'Aye aye.
Roger, that is. Top hole. We *are* up high.
One rather thinks that one might try a bunt.'
The voice cried out:
                    'Not now, you stupid . . .'
                                                Stunt

Upon stunt proved the fledgling *Charles* to be
Endowed with an instinctive mastery
Of flight, as with the cello or with polo.
Within the week our hero had gone solo.
The *Prince* had found his element at last –
Alone, a long way up and moving fast.
He flew a *Phantom* at the full ten tons
Which is as quick as buckshot goes from guns.
At *Sandringham* his father shooting partridges

Was hip-deep in a heap of empty cartridges
When *Charles* streaked overhead without a sound –
And then a clap of thunder shook the ground.
The *Duke* looked up to watch his son cavort
And just this once he did not mind spoiled sport,
While in the shooting brake the *Queen* looked down,
Her face divided between fear and frown.
But *Charles* was far already out of reach
And, twice as fast as cautionary speech
Can travel through the air, was on the climb.
He let the Earth spin round him all the time
Until he was as high as you can go
And still come back. He felt his own blood flow.
He heard his heart. His breath was like a storm.
He felt he was a god in human form.
If only he had not been cursed by birth
To spend his every waking day on Earth
He could have made his life up here in space!
He tapped the visor that concealed his face
And blessed it for the way it left him free
To taste the joys of anonymity.
Then he came down to be awarded wings.
The wings, along with several other things,
Went on his chest, which also boasted anchors,
Crossed parachutes, embroidered supertankers
And comparable insignia from all
The services. He had them wall to wall.
He wore a fore-and-after Admiral's hat
On top of which impressively there sat
A full Field Marshal's cap sporting a pair
Of pilot's goggles. Reading down from there
You found *Prince Charles* to be Colonel in Chief
Of Foot Guards, Fire Brigades and Flood Relief.
His belt was hung not just with swords and pistols
But plastic bags of breathalyser crystals
Denoting his high office in the Police.
His flying boots were lined with golden fleece
And came equipped with spurs. As was the rule
He slow-marched out past the assembled school

And off to *Windsor*, where *Grandfather*'s brother
Now lay in death. On orders from his mother
He met the *Duchess* at the castle gate.
'You'd think he'd never been your Head of State,'
She sighed through her black veil.

                                     'It's just so cheap
That he's not in the *Abbey*. I could weep.
Your *Grandmother*'s to blame. She hurts my pride
Just any way she can. Let's go inside.
I did the flowers myself. You see that smile?
He's doing that for me. That was his style.
I guess for me he'd do most anything.
That's why they had to stop him being *King*.
They made him feel that it was them or me.
It was because I gave him Liberty.'
Regaled with such a salad of strange notions
The future *King* fell prey to mixed emotions.
How could he let this poor sad creature know
That what she said was only partly so
And all irrelevant? One had no choice.
All he could do was ask in a soft voice:
'Have you come far?'

                               She had indeed, and yet
One sensed she'd gone as far as she would get.
Charles left the chapel. In his *Aston Martin*
He found a large beribboned cardboard carton
Marked 'Fragile'. When he ripped the wrappings off it
The sight inside redounded to his profit.
It was a crate of *Guinness* girls, each richer
Than *Croesus* and as pretty as a picture.
They had names like *Anita* and *Sabrina*.
The one that kissed him like a vacuum cleaner
Was probably *Sabrina*, since *Anita*
Burned steadily like an immersion heater,
Unless he'd mixed them both up with *Miranda*
Who seemed less keen to talk about *Uganda*.
There were four more at least by his rough count
And all in all it seemed a large amount
Of good luck to be having all at once,

(76)

But *Charles* by now was much less of a dunce
In matters amorous, and knew just what
To do and, more importantly, what not.
Indeed these days he went out every night.
Impressionable hearts broke left and right.
Davinas and *Amandas* ran with throbbing
Aortas toward him and retreated sobbing.
Both the *Biancas*, all the *Bonbon-Carters*
Came flying at his head with snapping garters.
Most he threw back. The nicest ones he kept,
But later if not sooner they all wept.
The *Queen*'s Lady in Waiting disapproved.
Eventually the *Queen* herself was moved
To utter remonstrances.

                     'We are grieved
To see these poor young women thus deceived.
From base activities you must desist
And aim for high-born names. Here is a list.'
Abashed, *Charles* trotted off with dogged loyalty
To check out *Europe*'s range of nubile Royalty.
Marie-Astrid? Their lunch was like a wake.
Monaco's *Caroline* was a mistake.
Marie-Astrid just sat there looking numb
And *Caroline* was either deaf and dumb
Or cowed by her cool mother *Princess Grace*.
Charles waved his hand before her pretty face
To see what it would take to make her think
Of something new to say, or just to blink.
She stared right through him at *Philippe Nouveau*.
The mismatch that resulted goes to show
How even at high level hearts rule heads
And strange bedfellows land in Royal beds.
Schloss after castle, *château* after court
Charles drew a blank. The list was growing short.
The last name on it drew him from the Old
World to the New. His Royal blood ran cold
When PRESIDENT NICK DIXON introduced
His daughter *Tricia*. The poor girl unloosed
A melting smile while *Dixon* chose a tape

(79)

For them to dance to. There seemed no escape
But luckily the sound that filled the room
Was less the voice of *Venus* than of Doom.
'You guys will have to deep-six the hot dough.
The rest of you can ditch the cars and blow.
We'll need a lucky break to beat this rap.
We're still up to our eyeballs in the . . .'

                                      Zap
Went the machine as *Dixon* switched it off –
A noise compounded by his nervous cough.
'I'll leave',
            he fondly said,
                        'you two alone
To get acquainted. Don't answer the phone.
Or if you do just tell them I'm not here.'
And out he went only to reappear
Upon the instant.
                  'Goddam closet door,
It always fools me. You two just ignore
My presence while I crouch behind this chair.
I'll keep real quiet. You won't know I'm there.'
'They paying you enough?'
                        asked *Charles*, employing
A trick to stop the conversation cloying
That *Uncle Dickie* said worked with the Yanks.
But *Dixon* was half-hidden behind banks
Of cushions and expressed no clear reply
Beyond a haunted shifting of one eye.
The salient fact was plain as *Tricia*'s face –
The transatlantic match would not take place.
From outside on the lawn a starter motor
Was heard, and then twin turbines and a rotor.
Charles ducked out through the down-wash, climbed
   aboard
And nodded to the pilot. Off they soared
While Tricia stood as wind-blown and forlorn
And lost as *Ruth* amid the alien corn.

BOOK NINE

I n moments snatched between official duties
Charles squired an endless string of casual beauties.
Canoes-full of them called for him in *Suva*.
He had them by the van-load in *Vancouver*.
Samoan soft hands filled his cup of kava.
He was the almond of their eyes in *Java*.
But never once did he neglect his role.
The Union Jack came twitching down the pole
In country after country. *Charles* saluted.
The local navy fired its gun and hooted
And up went the exotic square of rag
Henceforth to be the new-born nation's flag.
The *Empire* was no more, yet more than ever
Its quondam members appeared loath to sever
Their old alliance with the *British* throne.
The *Queen* sat solid on the Stone of *Scone* –
Or, as they say in *Scotland*, Stoon of *Scoon* –
And showed, while men walked weightless on the
    Moon,
That though the world was made of changing stuff
Enough, in her opinion, was enough.
Some things were simply best left as they were –
The very foremost of them being her.
On TV she announced her *Jubilee*.
'Good evening, everybody. This is we.
We think it meet to roundly celebrate
Our quarter century as Head of State.
Let joy be unconfined and hearts be large.
Our son the *Prince of Wales* will be in charge.
May all our subjects be with mirth infused.
Astonish us. We wish to be amused.'
She made the Royal gesture and dissolved.
The ghostly image rapidly revolved

And turned into the *Prince*, who cleared his throat
Before, as always, striking the right note.
'One finds oneself faced with the cheerful task
Of having as much fun as one could ask.
Particularly one looks forward to
The clever things that will be done by you.
There will be candy floss and pony rides
And cries of rapture rising from all sides.
You ladies will no doubt be baking cakes.
Let's show the world we've still got what it takes.
One will be glad to answer any questions.
Don't hesitate to send in your suggestions.'
That night so many bonfires were ablaze
Next day the land lay drowned in a thick haze.
A man called *Willy Hecklethrone, MP*
Denounced it all as Sheer Insanity,
A Suicidal Wallow in Nostalgia.
He might have been complaining of neuralgia
For all the notice anybody took.
The people either craned their necks to look
Or put up cardboard periscopes. *Fleet Street*
Was crammed ten deep each side. Between their feet
El Vino's journalistic clientele
Crawled feeling more than usually unwell
As down the smooth and sawdust-strewn macadam
Came rolling the great golden wheels of *Madam*.
She gave the Royal Wave. Beside her sat
Prince Philip in a rather terrific hat,
But their collective splendour was outshone
By him who rode behind. Their eldest son,
Clad in the uniforms of all three forces,
Stood in a boat drawn by a team of horses,
A scout car, a light aircraft and a tank.
Since no one else now equalled him in rank
He gave himself new medals by the box.
A busy batman pinned them on his socks,
There being nowhere else to put the things –
Such is the bric-à-brac that burdens kings.
The crowds cheered the parade up *Ludgate Hill*

To where *St Paul's* disgorged its overspill
Of droning clerics. Waiting in the nave
ARCHBISHOP COGWHEEL was all set to rave.
His chance to show the *Queen* how he adored her
Had come. For what seemed half a day he bored her
And all the waiting world with such a spiel
As made death a release and time unreal.
'Yea, blessed we are,'
                              he moaned,
                                        'we are thrice blessed.
Nay, four times . . .'
                         But let's spare ourselves the rest
And switch to the live coverage on TV
On which the first familiar face we see
Is MALCOLM MOTHERMILK.
                                 'One's simply staggered.
The scale of self-delusion leaves one haggard.
How can these people carry on this farce?
The final triumph of the middle class
Is surely this collective form of madness.
The whole thing fills me with a piercing sadness.
And listen to that poor wet bleating snob
Who calls himself *Archbishop*. One could sob.
The *Queen* looks ready to do something drastic.'
But DAVID DROSS thought otherwise.
                                         'Fantastic,
Amazing, super, marvellous, what a show,
Good evening, welcome, fabulous, hello.
The *Queen* looks stunned by all this eloquence.
She looks down at her lap. You get the sense
She finds the sermon fabulous, amazing,
Fantastic, super, welcome . . .'
                                 Glasses blazing,
The face of ALAN WHANKER filled the screen.
'The cool, crowned, cutie-pie we call the *Queen*
Caught in a candid close-up. Is she tired?
The drive of duty which once fiercely fired
That frail form finally now fades and fails.
The world looks to the wonder-boy from *Wales*

(85)

And wonders: will she fall out in his favour?
A succulent scenario to savour.
But while her son stays single, sources say,
The word on Abdication is: no way.'
The *Queen* slept soundly through *Cogwheel*'s oration
And woke refreshed to rule her grateful Nation
Until such time, at least, as *Charles* should choose
A consort congruent with her strict views
Of suitability. Meanwhile the *Prince*
Continued to ignore familial hints
And went on taking out the kind of girl
Who would have made his mother's top lip curl
Had that appendage been less disciplined.
But now a big event was in the wind –
The *Prince*'s Thirtieth Birthday Banquet Ball.
Home came the far-flung Royals one and all
To where, inside *Buck House*, a four-star feast –
Enough for twenty thousand guests at least –
A welter of gold plate and silver vessels –
On groaning boards laid out on creaking trestles –
Awaited them and all the Family Firm
Plus everybody worthy of the term
Celebrity, drawn from all social levels
By ST-JOHN STILTHEELS, Master of the Revels,
Who with pomade brushed through his flopping locks,
In buckled shoes and poised his pouncet box,
Now made a leg and swept his free hand wide
And nose-dived like a fawn shot in mid-stride
To greet the *Queen*.
                      'What *is* that thing you're wearing?'
She asked.
              'We find its neckline *far* too daring.'
His answer came from well below her knees.
'I'm clad in *Queen Victoria*'s chemise,
Your Majesty, the better to pronounce
My love for every frippery and flounce
Comprised in the great nosegay of Regality.
Apparelled thus, I flaunt my partiality.'

(87)

'*Stiltheels*, arise,'
                    she said.
                                        'You have done well.
We would sit down. Our bunions hurt like Hell.'
The whole vast company sat down to dine.
Charles heard a voice.
                                    'You're going to like the wine,'
Said *Kerry*.
                        'There's some more out in the truck.
Good *Aussie* stuff. None of that dago muck.
I trod the grapes myself only last week.
These poofters'll end up too pissed to speak.
Cop this black tie of mine. It's lizard skin.
Are all these sheilas yours? You're in like *Flynn*.'
And off lurched *Kerry* to his lowly place
As straight away the grand event gained pace.
From famous mouths too many to be counted
The decibels of conversation mounted.
The *Three Degrees* were fending off the *Goons*
While *Brezhnev* and *Giscard* were stealing spoons.
To do this neither of them used both hands
Unlike *Prince Bernhard* of the *Netherlands*.
And *Willy Brandt* had brought some *Russian* spies
Of whom one was *Lord Lucan* in disguise,
And *Lady Hardhart* sat with *Helmut Schmidt*
And both found *Jimmy Goldcap* a great wit,
Hardhart because she thought him Buccaneering
And *Schmidt* because of being hard of hearing.
Lord Lambchop sat with his new concubine
Who once was mistress to a friend of mine
Called *Perry Prykke*. Her name was *Anna Pest*.
Lovely she was, but *Lambchop* with grim zest
Was courting *Lady Highrise* of the *Towers*,
A prize past even his seductive powers.
And there was *Angie Ripemov* reciting
The menu while across from her sat writing
Tina von Braun, whose magazine the *Tittler*
Each month made her head bigger and name littler.
And all the daughters of my *Lady Freesia*

(88)

Shone in their different stunning ways, but easier
Than saying how they vied with one another
Is just to say they took after their mother.
And *Harold Half-pint* sat there looking harried
From being unsure whether he was married.
He paused and looked around him in a daze
As if attending one of his own plays.
And *Richard Inkwell* sat there in short pants
While *William Dens-Fogg*'s dim bifocal glance
Was vaguely drawn to *Hardy Aimhigh* bending
To measure inside legs. There was a rending
Cacophony as *Hardy*'s trousers split
With sheer excitement at the thrill of it,
Since every nether limb touched by his tape
Belonged to one whose high rank made him gape.
And *Dr Ownup* sat with *Shirley Whirley*.
Roy Junket was there too, but looking surly,
His Centre Party so slow to get going
It stumped him which direction it was growing.
Then MARGO HATBOX gave a little speech
For those admirers sitting within reach.
'Who's paying for this function? Is it us?
A matter that my Cabinet might discuss.
My goodness me, I hope *Stiltheels* has not
Splurged public funds. If so, then that's his lot.
The Public Sector needs a drastic trimming.
They're very good, these strawberries. And quite
    slimming.'
Beside *Lord Fatman*, *Baubles Hamstrung* sat –
And really, for that table, that was that –
And *Tito*'s head was lolling in his plate
Because the rest of him had come too late.
The *Gordons* were all there from *Duff* to *Hannah*
And all the *Fords* from *Gerald* down to *Anna*;
The *Soameses* were all there, *Enoch* to *Emma*;
The *Joneses* were there too – *Jack*, *Freddie*, *Gemma*,
Tom, *James*, *James-Earl*, *Ann*, *David*, *David Pryce*- –
I hope I haven't put the same *Jones* twice.
But now *Charles* in his favourite role as host

(90)

Rose up, told jokes, proposed the loyal toast,
Lit a cigar and called for the Court Fool,
A clown in cap and bells of the old school
Called JOHN-PAUL GINGER, who with rolling eyes,
Loose tights and long-toed shoes spoke in this wise:
'The *Prince* has played the mad-cap far too long.

He dresses up in ape suits like *King Kong*.
He talks in funny voices, wears false noses
And gets caught by the Press in awkward poses
With naked girls on ski-slopes in *Australia*
Or on *Swiss* beaches. *Britain* faces failure
And all we let this young man do is wank.
He should be put in charge of the Think Tank!
His present unemployment is absurd.
It ill becomes the future *Charles III*.
I am the ideal person to advise him.
Give him to me and you won't recognise him.'
The roars of mirth that greeted *Ginger*'s act
Were joined in by the *Prince*, who'd not in fact
Spent one day in three decades being idle
And half the time felt close to suicidal
At how his life was planned to the last minute
With very little room for Wanking in it.
Enough. By now the party was alight.
The sound of broken glass assailed the night
As in through the French windows *Princess Anne*
Came bursting on a prancing horse. The man
Who'd won her heart was at her heaving flank,
Her equine equal though of lower rank.
Above the uproar the familiar keening
Of DORLING WHITHERS brought out the full
  meaning.
'The *Princess* and *Mark Pillocks* side by side,
And with what stateliness this couple ride.
They're jumping all the tables one by one,
Anne mounted on *Yoshiba Rising Sun
Electric Hairdryer* and *Mark*, of course,
In charge of that most spirited young horse
Hitachi Automatic Bathroom Scales.
And now with what authority *Mark* sails
Out of the saddle into that tureen
And disappears. Well! Never have I seen
A jump-orf like it. *Anne* gives a great whoop
To see *Mark* drenched from head to foot in soup,
And she's orf too! She's gone! Ooh! Oh, I say!

She's upside down and hits the *crème brûlée*
A mighty smack! She's broken through the crust
And now she's surfaced snorting with disgust.
She's flinging bits of custard everywhere
And most of them in *Princess Michael*'s hair.'
But *Princess Michael*'s intricate coiffure
Retained undimmed its glittering allure.
The custard-blobs were lost among the pearls
Already pinned into the twists and twirls
And braided loops that crowned her noble cranium
Like an atomic model of uranium.
Mayhem had broken loose. Young bloods were pelting
The older guests with ice-cream, which was melting.
Dick Jiggle and the *Bleeding Gits* were playing.
The standard of behaviour was decaying.
The carpets were rolled back. The dancing started.
Dick Jiggle yelled like someone being martyred
Who'd changed his mind, while every bright young
    eligible
Sprang forward squealing something unintelligible.
The hunt was up. The *Queen* kicked off her shoes.
Nikon told *Charles*:
                              'It's time for you to choose.
They're all here and they're all leaping about.
This is your chance to pick the right one out.
Remember, though: the girl you make your wife
Will lead what no sane dog would call a life.
So pick one who's got infinite reserves
Of gravity and disc-brakes on her nerves.
You want a quiet one without a past.
A slow enough start and the thing might last.
Look through the crowd. Just let your instinct guide
    you.
Somebody here will spend her life beside you
With no way back, no sudden change of heart,
No clearing of the decks for a fresh start
Or even pause for thought. Look for the eyes
Which with their sadness seem to recognise
That shared with you the future is as set

(96)

As concrete. Look for well-controlled regret.'
Charles looked. His glance flew through the writhing
   tangle
Of sweating bodies bent at every angle
And settled on someone who seemed content
To stand and be amused by how things went.
He'd known her all her life, but no one knows
The value of the quality Repose
Until the day, which should not come too soon
Or too late (from a gold-sprayed fruit festoon
He plucked an apple), when excitement bores him
And worldliness, though all the world adores him,
Seems childish. *Charles* bent down and smoothly
   rolled
Along the floor that fateful blob of gold.
The girls we've mentioned would have looked aghast
To see its aureate plumpness trundle past,
But they saw nothing. Only *Lady Jane*
Looked down and winced with what might have been
   pain.
Not even *Farrah Fawcett-Downwards* saw it
Who had the teeth to pick it up and gnaw it
Even had it been solid. When it stopped
It stopped below a shy gaze that had dropped
To meet it long before it started rolling –
A fact the also-rans might find consoling,
Since often, in defeat, it helps to know
That Destiny decreed what should be so.
And so, as all the dancers leapt and whooped,
Lady Diana Seethrough-Spiffing stooped
And gingerly picked up the shining treasure
With what looked more like thoughtfulness than
   pleasure.
'Jeez, mate,'
       said *Kerry*,
            'Got to hand it to you.
You don't need much help with the sheilas, do you?
That one you bowled to should be keeping wicket.
You think she might consider playing cricket?'

(99)

BOOK TEN

*P**rince*, ballads used to end with a direct
  Address to their grand object of respect,
So why not epics too? *Horse Guards* in summer
Rings to the quick-fire of the calling drummer.
The massed band strikes up '*British Grenadiers*',
The Chelsea Pensioners blink back their tears,
The Escort moves out smartly to receive
The Colour. Even those who don't believe
In ghosts must see them here. The regiments
March past in both the past and present tense.
Their shadows tremble in the metal hail
That fell sideways waist-high at *Passchendaele*.
Their step calls up the roar of tasselled shields
Rattled by assegais. The battlefields
Are joined beneath their feet like a long road
Green in the distance from the blood that's flowed,
And still they march, and would march on their
    knees,
And waiting for them are the *Japanese*
Who blaze away from all sides without stopping,
Zooms zooming, shutters snapping, flashbulbs
    popping.
The Colour swerves and dips. The *Queen* salutes.
A horse with *Uncle Dickie*'s empty boots
Stuck backwards in its stirrups paws the gravel.
Gladly I leave you to that cruel time travel
In which no new occurrence can be changed
By you or you by it – it's all arranged.
Your bearskin looks as if it weighs a ton.
The crown will weigh more. How could anyone
Believe you lead a leisured life? But then
Like most who make their living by the pen
I have a tendency to patronise

All those with steady jobs. I sympathise
With your position but I'm glad it's you
That's in it and that what you're bound to do
You do with some style and do not look haunted
By sombre Fate or even mildly daunted.
I take you for a man. You're not divine.
Your feet, I think, smell pretty much like mine
Although made from a finer grade of clay.
And yet it seems to me the Throne today
Works as it always has to incarnate
Tradition and thus make it serve the State.
I am a Monarchist through lack of trust
In human rationality, which must
Be kept in bounds like any other force
Or else, if it's allowed to run its course,
It can and will work mischief in a fashion
Beyond the maddest daydreams of blind passion.
The two most murderous of modern nations
Had this in common – they were innovations.
Men thought them up. Time's heritage was mocked
And all the worst hobgoblins were unlocked,
Since only the collective evolution
Of custom, language, law and institution
Can tame that impulse in the human soul
Whose awful vigour helps to make it whole.
Tradition's tamed you too. Thank *God* for that.
With *Fleet Street* talking through its tasteless hat
You must have felt like killing and been glad
Not to possess what once you would have had –
The power to silence any saucy voice
By edifying methods of your choice.
In those days, had I written this, cropped ears,
A slit nose and a stretch of twenty years
(Or on the rack) might well have been my lot –
Unless I was unfortunate and got
Some stiffer penalty, such as my head
Subtracted from my trunk and put instead
On *London Bridge*. I'm glad you're not allowed
To do that to me. But though not endowed

(102)

With all the old prerogatives, you've still
Some room to implement your Royal will –
Your attitude will have its influence
And even when you can't much shape events
You can be sure that they'd be otherwise
Without your being there to exercise
Your foremost function, which is to deny
Anyone else the chance to deify
Himself and rule unchecked and say 'The State
Is Me' and so go mad through growing great.
Some say you lack imagination. They
Do not twig that the unexcited way
You go about your business is the proof
That if we pay someone to stay aloof
And be symbolic we do best to use
The privilege History's given us and choose
A Family Firm who'll make sure that the crown
Lands on a level head when it's passed down.
The Colour's trooped. This ceremony ends
And for the next one your friend *Kerry* sends
A note conveying his best wishes. He
Was shy enough to seek some help from me
Since this is his first venture in verse form.
I find his effort lyrical and warm –
Imbued, indeed, with that raw tenderness
Only a primitive can well express.
'Dear *Chunder*, When you two have tied the knot
Try not to spend the whole day in the cot.
Remember your old mates in th'*Austral* isle
Who'd like to take a dekko at your dial
From time to time. Tell *Di* that red-backs lurk
Even beneath the throne. I'm hard at work
Digging latrines at school. Meanwhile I'll post
Some more food parcels. I don't like to boast
But when I think I helped you find your feet
I hum with pride like blowies on fresh meat.
Di might have had a poofter to look after –
Which would have been a cause of hollow laughter
Among red-blooded *Aussies* to whom she

(103)

Is no ice-cold Pom sheila obviously.
Well, sport, I'll bring my poem to an end.
Don't let them come the raw prawn. Signed, A
    Friend.'
By now it's time my poem ended too.
It does so with my compliments to you
And everything the words 'Good luck' can mean.
God bless the *Prince* of *Wales*.

GOD SAVE THE QUEEN